Essentials in Writing Level 3
Second Edition
Assessment/Resource Booklet

Authors
Matthew Stephens
Athena Lester
Danielle Nettleton
Hope Tolbert

Teacher
Matthew Stephens

Senior Consultant
Mary McGee

Designer
Boston Stephens

Project Coordinator
Athena Lester

Editor
Athena Lester

info@essentialsinwriting.com
www.essentialsinwriting.com
Copyright © 2020 by Matthew B. Stephens

All rights reserved. No part of this book may be reproduced or transmitted in any form by any means – electronic, mechanical, photocopying, recording, or otherwise.

Printed in the United States of America
Update December 2023

A note about assessment point values:

Teachers are encouraged to use their own point values/scoring system, but if you prefer, you are welcome to use the point values suggested for each assessment. Generally, point values for each kind of activity correspond to the equivalent activity in the student book.

- Identify activities: 1 point each
- Apply activities: 2 points each
- Activities involving identifying items or errors in a paragraph: 1 point per error/item

TABLE OF CONTENTS

ASSESSMENTS

Assessment 1 – Complete Subjects, Simple Subjects, Complete Predicates, & Simple Predicates (Lessons 2-5) 4

Assessment 2 – Complete and Incomplete Sentences, & Types of Sentences and Punctuation Marks (Lessons 6-7) 6

Assessment 3 – Common and Proper Nouns, & Singular and Plural Nouns (Lessons 8-9) 8

Assessment 4 – Pronouns and Antecedents (Lesson 10) 10

Assessment 5 – Singular Possessive Nouns, Plural Possessive Nouns, & More Plural Possessive Nouns (Lessons 11-13) 12

Assessment 6 – Adjectives (Lesson 14) 14

Assessment 7 – Action Verbs; Present, Past, and Future Tense Action Verbs, Irregular Action Verbs; Linking Verbs; & Present, Past, and Future Tense Linking Verbs (Lessons 15-19) 16

Assessment 8 – Adverbs That Modify Verbs (Lesson 20) 18

Assessment 9 – Pronoun/Antecedent Agreement (Lesson 21) 20

Assessment 10 – Subject/Verb Agreement (Lesson 22) 22

Assessment 11 – Contractions & Don't/Doesn't Problem (Lessons 23-24) 24

Assessment 12 – Writing Items in a Series (Lesson 28) 26

Assessment 13 – Simple and Compound Sentences (Lesson 29) 28

Assessment 14 – Incomplete Sentences & Run-On Sentences (Lessons 30-31) 30

Unit 1 Comprehensive Assessment (Lessons 2-31) 32

Assessment 15 – The Writing Process (Lessons 32-37) 36

Assessment 16 – Paragraphs (Lessons 38-43) 40

Assessment 17 – Expository Writing (Lessons 44-53) 44

Assessment 18 – Persuasive Writing (Lessons 54-63) 50

Assessment 19 – Descriptive Writing (Lessons 64-73) 56

Unit 2 Comprehensive Assessment (Lessons 32-73) 62

RESOURCES 66

ASSESSMENT ANSWER KEY 127

Assessments

ASSESSMENT

_____ / 62 points

Assessment 1 – Complete Subjects, Simple Subjects, Complete Predicates, & Simple Predicates (Lessons 2-5)

A. Complete the sentence with your own *simple subject*.

1. _____ dove into the water.

2. _____ flew across the sky.

3. _____ likes pink lemonade.

4. _____ smell delicious.

5. _____ rode a camel.

6. _____ made s'mores.

B. Complete the sentence with your own *simple predicate*.

1. Her friend _____.

2. The tree _____.

3. The ball _____.

4. My grandma _____.

5. The snake _____.

6. Their pets _____.

C. Complete each sentence with a *subject* or a *predicate*.

_____ had a birthday party. Her friends and family _____. _____ ate cake and ice cream. At the party, she _____. _____ received many gifts. Everyone _____.

4

ASSESSMENT

D. Circle the *simple subject* and underline the *simple predicate* in each sentence.

1. My family hosted a barbeque.
2. Mom grilled the hamburgers and hotdogs.
3. Dad made coleslaw and baked beans.
4. Grandma made homemade ice cream.
5. My cousins and I played games together.
6. We watched the fireworks.
7. The fireworks looked dazzling.
8. Everyone left late at night.
9. I dreamed about the fireworks.
10. The barbeque was a fun event.

E. Circle the *complete subject* in each sentence.

1. The boy in the blue shirt shared his cookie.
2. Dad went to the store today.
3. The man in the suit opened the door for us.
4. The orange kitten hides under the bed.
5. The woman in the red gown spilled her drink.
6. All the chipmunks scampered away.
7. That chubby puppy is very cuddly.
8. Martin walked three miles.

F. Underline the *complete predicate* in each sentence.

1. Desiree wrote a story about talking ladybugs.
2. We danced in the rain.
3. I dreamed about a scary monster.
4. Laura rode on the big roller coaster.
5. The dog knows many tricks.
6. I watched a movie about dinosaurs.
7. Shyla planted trees for a school project.
8. Our family looked at the Christmas lights.

ASSESSMENT

_____ / 42 points

Assessment 2 – Complete and Incomplete Sentences, & Types of Sentences and Punctuation Marks (Lessons 6-7)

A. The following sentences are missing either a *subject* or a *predicate*. Complete each sentence with a subject or a predicate.

1. The _____ laughed loudly.

2. The dentist _____ at the patient's teeth.

3. The _____ published a book.

4. Danny _____ the guitar.

5. Flora _____ at the talent show.

6. Our family _____ homemade pizzas every Saturday night.

7. _____ lifts heavy weights.

B. Write whether each sentence is *declarative, interrogative, exclamatory,* or *imperative*.

1. Are you wearing new shoes? _____

2. I love llamas! _____

3. Sarah is allergic to peanuts. _____

4. Don't eat the brownies. _____

5. Do you want a ride? _____

6. Wait for me! _____

7. Tigers have stripes. _____

8. Read this book. _____

9. I won the contest! _____

10. Don't run in the halls! _____

ASSESSMENT

C. Underline the *complete sentences* and circle the *incomplete sentences* below.

1. I took the trash out.

2. The snow fell outside.

3. Held the baby.

4. The broken cup.

5. We packed for vacation.

6. The cupcake.

7. Her lizard eats grasshoppers.

8. Their puppy.

D. The sentences have mistakes in punctuation. Rewrite the sentence with correct punctuation.

1. Brush your teeth

_____

2. Are you ready

_____

3. Let's play outside

_____

4. Did you do the dishes

_____

5. Eat your vegetables

_____

ASSESSMENT

_____ / 79 points

Assessment 3 – Common and Proper Nouns, & Singular and Plural Nouns (Lessons 8-9)

A. Circle each *proper noun*.

1. Michael Jackson was a pop star.
2. He was born in Gary, Indiana, in August.
3. Michael Jackson was part of a band called the Jackson 5.
4. He is known as the King of Pop.
5. Michael invented dance moves.

B. Underline each *common noun*.

1. Rose and I walked to the park.
2. We swung on the swings and went down the slide.
3. I brought granola bars for a snack.
4. I gave Rose one granola bar.
5. Evan walked into the park.

C. Fill in the blank with your own *proper noun*.

1. We flew to _____ for vacation. (*Place*)
2. I have a friend named _____. (*Person*)
3. _____ is my cousin. (*Person*)
4. _____ is a country. (*Place*)
5. _____ was a president. (*Person*)

D. Fill in the blank with your own *common noun*.

1. The _____ walked into the building. (*Person*)
2. I lost my _____. (*Thing*)
3. Our family went to the _____. (*Place*)

ASSESSMENT

E. Underline the *common nouns* and circle the *proper nouns*.

1. tiger
2. Betsy Ross
3. rose
4. medicine
5. Lucy Ball
6. galaxy
7. Brazil
8. happiness
9. Rebekah
10. California
11. Martin Luther King
12. American Music Award
13. New York
14. notebook
15. yellow

F. Underline each *common noun* and circle each *proper noun* in the paragraph.

Harry made a new friend named Charlie. They have class with Mrs. Robinson. They met at lunch. Harry and Charlie had sandwiches and chips. They ate at the same table. Harry and Charlie played at recess. They climbed the monkey bars and slid down the slide. They played tag with Donte. Harry and Charlie are glad they are friends.

G. Underline the *singular nouns* and circle the *plural nouns* below.

1. The teacher likes her students.
2. There are muddy footprints all over the floor.
3. Jenna runs fast through the forest.
4. The mountains have huge trees.
5. Trey washes the dishes in the sink.

H. Fill in the blank with the *plural* of the indicated noun.

1. The _____ play in the backyard. (*child*)
2. The _____ laughed and told stories. (*woman*)
3. My _____ and I sat at the front row of the concert! (*friend*)
4. The _____ look like a dinosaur in the sky. (*cloud*)
5. The repairman fixed the broken _____. (*light*)
6. My grandma baked a lot of _____. (*cookie*)

ASSESSMENT

_____ / 29 points

Assessment 4 – Pronouns and Antecedents (Lesson 10)

A. Underline the *pronouns*.

1. Ariana caught the baseball. She is good at baseball.

2. Ryan performed a dance. He is graceful.

3. Liz shared her cookie with me. I was so happy!

4. Luke went on vacation to Canada. He told us all about it.

B. Circle the *antecedents*.

1. Our family put up the Christmas tree. We think it is pretty!

2. Josephine has a test tomorrow. She has to study hard for it.

3. The cat hissed at the dog. The dog ran away from it.

4. The watch broke. The watchmaker will fix it.

C. Rewrite the sentences and replace the underlined nouns with the correct *pronouns*.

1. Tammy told Steve that <u>Steve's</u> cherry pie was the best she ever had.

_____

2. Zara stayed up until midnight writing <u>Zara's</u> paper.

_____

3. The dog likes playing with the <u>dog's</u> toys.

_____

4. Maria has to do <u>Maria's</u> chores before going to bed.

_____

D. Underline the *pronouns* and circle the *antecedents* in the paragraph below.

Jacob and Josiah are twins! They both enjoy dancing. They are good at it! Jacob likes to dance ballet. Josiah likes to dance hip hop. They go to a dance studio almost every day. The teachers think they are talented. They want Jacob and Josiah want to go to dance school someday. Jacob and Josiah are excited for the future!

ASSESSMENT

ASSESSMENT

_____ / 24 points

Assessment 5 – Singular Possessive Nouns, Plural Possessive Nouns, & More Plural Possessive Nouns (Lessons 11-13)

A. Use *singular possessive nouns* to shorten the phrases.

1. the eraser of the pencil　　_____

2. the sleeve of the shirt　　_____

3. the sole of the shoe　　_____

4. the feather of the bird　　_____

B. Use *plural possessive nouns* to shorten the phrases.

1. the presents of the families　　_____

2. the candy of the kids　　_____

3. the songs of the men　　_____

4. the honey of the bees　　_____

C. Combine the sentences using a *singular possessive noun*.

1. The plaid shirt looked nice. The plaid shirt belonged to Drake.

_____

2. The restaurant was busy. The restaurant belonged to Danae.

_____

D. Combine the sentences using a *plural possessive noun*.

1. The books fell. The books belonged to the shelves.

_____

2. The dresses were pretty. The dresses belonged to the seamstresses.

_____

ASSESSMENT

ASSESSMENT

_____ / 35 points

Assessment 6 – Adjectives (Lesson 14)

A. Underline the *adjectives* in these sentences.

1. The strong wind whipped my hair.
2. The calm cats purred on my lap.
3. Mom flipped the burnt pancakes in the pan.
4. The delicious ice cream cone dripped on my arm.
5. We drove past the bright lights of the big city.
7. The fluffy pillows lie on the soft bed.
8. Dad put sunscreen on my pale skin.
9. The nervous speaker walked to the stage.
10. My silly uncle told a lot of funny jokes.

B. Complete each sentence with an *adjective*.

1. The sweater feels _____.

2. I thought the book was very _____.

3. Mom's lotion smells _____.

4. The _____ bull ran at the man.

5. The _____ plate shattered into pieces.

6. The _____ teacher taught the students math.

7. I held the _____ hamster.

C. Underline the *adjectives* in the paragraph below.

Vanessa plants tiny seeds in the brown soil. She works expertly in her vegetable garden. Vanessa grows purple eggplants, green cucumbers, and yellow squash. With the fresh vegetables, she makes delicious meals. Vanessa and her friends have a great time thinking of new recipes to use. She loves working in her garden and making different kinds of foods to eat and share.

14

ASSESSMENT

ASSESSMENT

_____ / 40 points

Assessment 7 – Action Verbs; Present, Past, and Future Tense Action Verbs; Irregular Action Verbs; Linking Verbs; & Present, Past, and Future Tense Linking Verbs (Lessons 15-19)

A. Underline each *action verb*.

1. A friendly dog belonged to a little girl.
2. The girl named the dog Bolt.
3. Then, she lost Bolt during a rainy day.
4. However, she found her favorite puppy at the park.

B. Complete each sentence with an *action verb*.

1. The horse _____ in the field.
2. Grandma _____ a sweater for Grandpa.
3. The baby _____ during the whole trip.
4. Uncle Albert _____ a funny story.

C. Write whether the underlined verbs are in the *past, present*, or *future tense*.

1. Dad <u>brews</u> coffee for Mom. _____
2. The birds <u>chirp</u> softly. _____
3. Faith <u>shared</u> her sundae with George. _____
4. The pants <u>ripped</u> at the knee. _____

D. Rewrite the sentences and change the *present tense* verbs to *past tense* verbs.

1. Angelica <u>drops</u> her toy in the bucket.

_____

2. Snow <u>falls</u> in winter.

_____

16

ASSESSMENT

E. Rewrite the sentences and change the *present tense* verbs to *future tense* verbs.

1. The punch <u>spills</u> on the floor.

_____

2. The couple <u>holds</u> hands.

_____

F. Underline each *linking verb*.

1. I am excited for the show!

2. This shirt is my lucky shirt.

3. Andrea was sick yesterday.

4. We are happy because it is the last day of school.

5. Jimmy and Matt were nervous for the test.

G. Write whether the underlined linking verbs are in the *past, present,* or *future tense*.

1. I <u>am</u> a good baseball player.   _____

2. Sarah <u>will be</u> next in line for lunch.   _____

3. You <u>were</u> really funny in the play.   _____

H. Rewrite the sentences to change the *present tense* linking verbs to *past tense* linking verbs.

1. Carol <u>is</u> a great singer.

_____

2. Mom and Dad <u>are</u> in the garage.

_____

I. Rewrite the sentences to change the *present tense* linking verbs to *future tense* linking verbs.

1. My turtle <u>is</u> in the swimming pool.

_____

2. I <u>am</u> a space explorer.

_____

ASSESSMENT

_____ / 29 points

Assessment 8 – Adverbs That Modify Verbs (Lesson 20)

A. Complete each sentence with your own *adverb*.

1. Melody _____ swam to the other side of the pool.

2. The zoo animals _____ slept at the end of the day.

3. The doctor _____ checked the patient.

4. My sister _____ finished her homework.

5. A little squirrel _____ came out of its hiding spot.

B. Underline each *adverb* in the sentences.

1. George nervously walked up onto the stage.
2. The snow softly fell to the ground.
3. Her book landed loudly after she dropped it.
4. Turtles don't always walk slowly.
5. My brother rarely cleans his room.
6. Carly did well on her test last Tuesday.

C. Underline each *adverb* in the paragraph.

Reindeer live in Alaska. Some people call them caribou. Some days, they playfully run around with each other. Reindeer eat grass daily. They can safely be in the snow all day. This is because they are completely covered with thick, warm fur. Their noses quickly warm up the air they breathe before it gets to their lungs. Reindeer are interesting animals!

D. Complete the paragraph with your own *adverbs*.

Josie _____ wrapped the present. She _____ placed it under the tree when she was finished. The toy for her brother would _____ excite her brother. They could play with the toy _____ all day. Josie's brother was going to be surprised on Christmas!

ASSESSMENT

ASSESSMENT

_____ / 30 points

Assessment 9 – Pronoun/Antecedent Agreement (Lesson 21)

A. Circle the *pronoun* that agrees with (or matches) the underlined antecedent.

1. Marshal washes (his / their) laundry on Saturdays.

2. The zookeeper forgot (her / its) hat at home.

3. Cows went to sleep in (their / his) barn.

4. In Casey's room, (she / her) found (her / its) socks.

5. Darla doesn't like (her / his) soup.

6. The dog wiped (its / their) paws on the mat.

7. Ariel swam in (her / its) pool all day.

8. The monkey picked bugs off (its / their) friend.

9. The doctor forgot (his / him) stethoscope.

10. I can't believe (I / my) shoes are already dirty.

B. Complete the sentences with *pronouns*. Use pronouns that agree with (or match) the underlined antecedents.

1. The dinosaur ate _____ food.

2. Joseph went to the beach in _____ Jeep. _____ saw sharks in the sea!

3. That kangaroo jumped so high, _____ head touched the tree branch!

4. Kelsey, Rick, and Thomas are siblings. _____ get along so well.

5. When Tyler lost _____ action figure, _____ cried all week.

6. Last year, I went to Disney World and met Minnie Mouse. _____ was so nice!

7. I saw a mother duck swimming in the pond. _____ had six babies with her!

8. Ryland and Denise ran a marathon. _____ were the first pair to finish!

9. My brother is a great writer. _____ won three awards last year.

10. At the dentist, my sister waited quietly. _____ got to choose a lollipop!

ASSESSMENT

ASSESSMENT

_____ / 26 points

Assessment 10 – Subject/Verb Agreement (Lesson 22)

A. Circle the *verb* that agrees with (or matches) the subject.

1. Lily (visit / visits) her grandma on Fridays.

2. They (like / likes) to read together.

3. They (bake / bakes) chocolate chip cookies.

4. Lily and her grandma (sing / sings) silly songs.

5. Her grandma (sits / sit) in a rocking chair.

6. Lily (rest / rests) on the carpet.

B. Fill in the blanks with verbs. Remember to match *singular subjects* with *singular verbs* and *plural subjects* with *plural verbs*!

1. Sheep _____ grass.

2. The vet _____ 24 animals.

3. My brothers _____ video games sometimes.

4. Snow _____ on the house.

5. The apples _____ off the tree.

6. Riley and Leslie _____ to the ice cream store.

7. Her pecan pies _____ delicious!

C. Circle the *subject* that agrees with (or matches) the verb.

1. (A squid / Squids) have huge eyes.

2. The (bear / bears) sleeps in the cave.

3. (Firemen / The fireman) works very hard.

4. The (plants / plant) is growing so tall!

5. (Cake / cakes) bakes in the oven.

6. The (forest / forests) is full of many trees.

ASSESSMENT

ASSESSMENT

_____ / 23 points

Assessment 11 – Contractions & Don't/Doesn't Problem (Lessons 23-24)

A. Underline the *contractions* in the sentences below. Write the two words that are being combined on the blanks.

1. You're not at home right now.   _____ _____

2. The turkeys don't fly very often.   _____ _____

3. She'd go to Tennessee if she could.   _____ _____

4. Aren't you going to the movie?   _____ _____

5. There's my lost shoe!   _____ _____

B. Rewrite the sentences and combine the two underlined words into a *contraction*.

1. <u>You have</u> been to Canada five times.

_____

2. Casey knows <u>I will</u> clean my room.

_____

3. <u>It is</u> going to be so fun going to the fair!

_____

4. My brother <u>will not</u> eat pickles.

_____

C. Write *don't* or *doesn't* to complete the sentence.

1. My cat _____ like eating tuna.

2. Charlie and Ann _____ go to musicals very often.

3. His friend _____ have to mow the lawn.

4. The bakers _____ always bake bread on Fridays.

5. Their swim coach _____ feel good today.

ASSESSMENT

ASSESSMENT

ASSESSMENT

_____ / 29 points

Assessment 12 – Writing Items in a Series (Lesson 28)

A. Add the missing *commas* to the *series* in the sentences below.

1. Twizzlers Skittles and Twix are my favorite candies.
2. My cousin has a cat a pig and a parrot.
3. We hiked biked and camped together.
4. They had spaghetti cheese and broccoli for dinner.
5. Did you read play or sleep?

B. Fill in the blanks below with nouns. Add the missing *commas*.

1. On vacation, we went to _____ _____ and _____.

2. My favorite animals are _____ _____ and _____.

3. They had _____ _____ and _____ at the restaurant.

4. Carol wrote a story about _____ _____ and _____.

5. _____ _____ and _____ are my friend's favorite flowers.

6. Delilah went to _____ _____ and _____.

C. Fill in the blanks below with verbs. Add the missing *commas*.

1. The puppies in the box _____ _____ and _____.

2. In the morning, birds _____ _____ and _____.

3. I _____ _____ and _____ at Grandma's house.

4. In the video game, you _____ _____ and _____.

5. The box _____ _____ and _____ down the steps.

6. Food _____ _____ and _____ on the grill.

ASSESSMENT

ASSESSMENT

_____ / 16 points

Assessment 14 – Incomplete Sentences & Run-On Sentences (Lessons 30-31)

A. The sentences below are *incomplete*. Write "S" if the sentences are missing a *subject* and "P" if they are missing a *predicate*.

1. The fruit snacks from my mother.   _____

2. My best friend Bella.   _____

3. Walked the dog across the park.   _____

4. My neighbor's cousin Timothy.   _____

B. Correct the *incomplete sentences* on the lines provided.

1. Nachos with cheese and salsa.

_____

2. Jumped into the freezing lake.

_____

C. Correct each *run-on sentence* by making it into two separate sentences. Don't forget to use *correct punctuation* and *capitalization*.

1. My dad likes sports his favorite is basketball.

_____

2. My cousin likes dragons he has three dragon costumes.

_____

D. Correct each *run-on sentence* by making it into a compound sentence. Don't forget to a *comma* and a *conjunction*.

1. Kenny got new boots they are very shiny.

_____

2. Krysta likes chips she eats them every day.

_____

ASSESSMENT

ASSESSMENT

_____ / 8 points

Assessment 15 – The Writing Process (Lessons 32-37)

Circle the letter next to the correct answer.

1. What is the correct order of the writing process?

    A. Revise, Brainstorm, Organize, Draft, Final Draft

    B. Draft, Brainstorm, Organize, Final Draft, Revise

    C. Organize, Draft, Brainstorm, Revise, Final Draft

    D. Brainstorm, Organize, Draft, Revise, Final Draft

2. *Brainstorming* is when you…

    A. make a plan.

    B. choose a topic.

    C. edit for errors.

    D. revise your draft.

3. What do you do when you create a *final draft*?

    A. Organize.

    B. Put your ideas in order.

    C. Edit your work and create a final copy.

    D. Revise.

4. When you *draft*, you should do all of the following except:

    A. use the information in your plan

    B. put your ideas into order

    C. make sure your writing is perfect the first time

    D. use complete sentences

To complete the assessment, complete the paragraph writing prompt on the following page.

36

ASSESSMENT

ASSESSMENT

Assessment 15 – The Writing Process (Lessons 32-37)

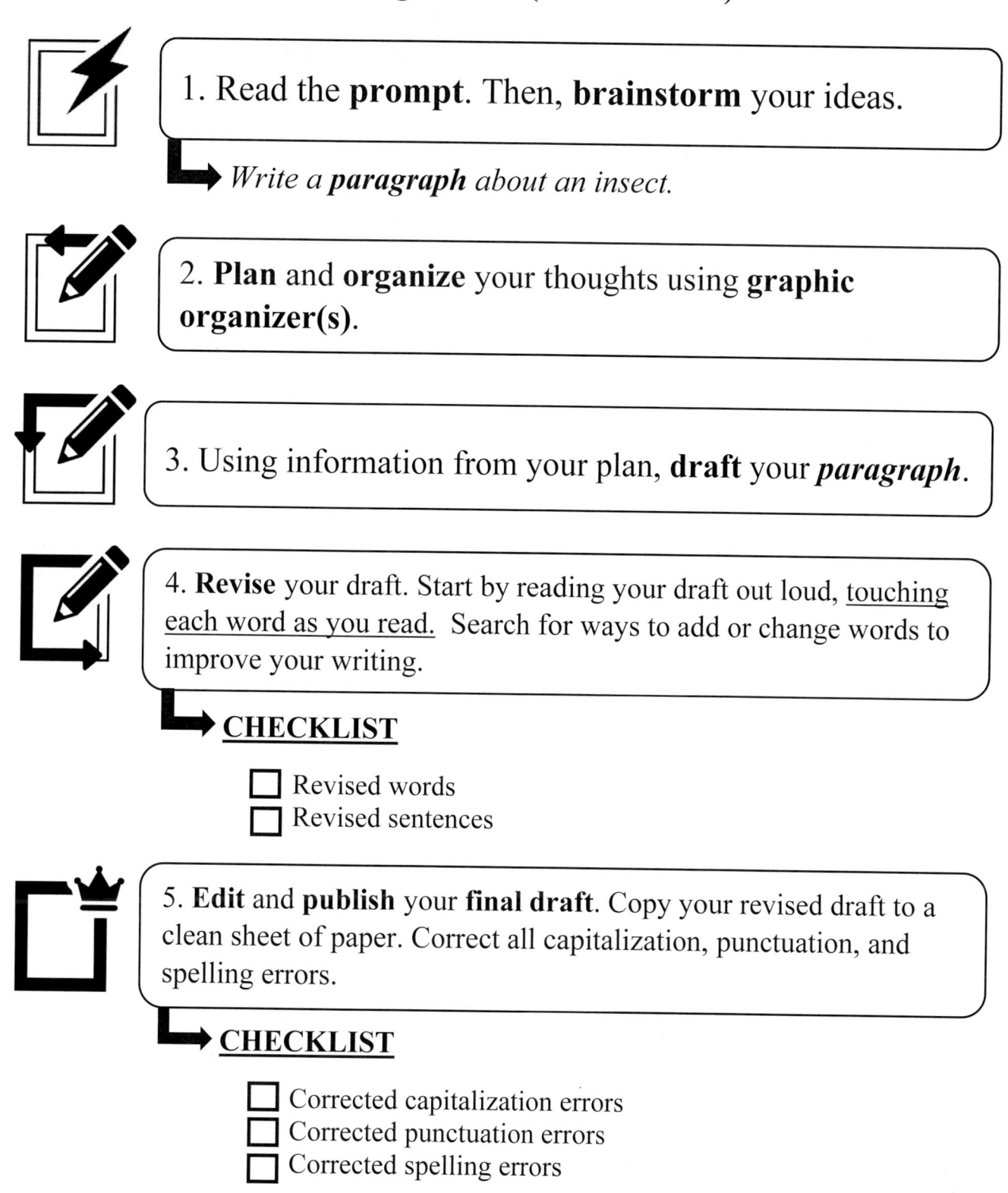

1. Read the **prompt**. Then, **brainstorm** your ideas.

   → *Write a **paragraph** about an insect.*

2. **Plan** and **organize** your thoughts using **graphic organizer(s)**.

3. Using information from your plan, **draft** your *paragraph*.

4. **Revise** your draft. Start by reading your draft out loud, <u>touching each word as you read.</u> Search for ways to add or change words to improve your writing.

   → **CHECKLIST**
   - ☐ Revised words
   - ☐ Revised sentences

5. **Edit** and **publish** your **final draft**. Copy your revised draft to a clean sheet of paper. Correct all capitalization, punctuation, and spelling errors.

   → **CHECKLIST**
   - ☐ Corrected capitalization errors
   - ☐ Corrected punctuation errors
   - ☐ Corrected spelling errors

ASSESSMENT

Paragraph Practice Checklist

I indented my opening sentence. ___/1

I wrote an opening sentence. ___/1

I wrote three or more body sentences. ___/1

I stayed on topic. ___/1

I wrote a closing sentence. ___/1

I checked my spelling. ___/1

I used capitalization correctly. ___/1

I used punctuation correctly. ___/1

My handwriting is neat, and my words are spaced correctly. ___/1

Remember, good writing takes practice!

Total Points: ___/9

ASSESSMENT

_____ / 6 points

Assessment 16 – Paragraphs (Lessons 38-43)

Circle the letter next to the correct answer.

1. Which of these is the best *opening sentence* for a paragraph about farms?

    A. That's everything I know about Alaska.

    B. Cows eat grass, hay, and oats.

    C. That day, we went to bed early.

    D. Many animals live on a farm.

Read the following paragraph:

Sea turtles lay their eggs on the beach. They can lay over 100 eggs at a time. I like cereal. Sea turtles have a soft shell. Mother sea turtles make a nest with their flippers. Sea turtles are neat.

2. Which body sentence does *not* stay on topic in the paragraph above?

    A. They can lay over 100 eggs at a time.

    B. I like cereal.

    C. Sea turtle eggs have a soft shell.

    D. Mother sea turtles make a nest with their flippers.

Read the following paragraph:

My family and I go to the pumpkin patch every year. My sister likes to find the biggest pumpkin there. I like the really small pumpkins. One year, my dad stepped on a pumpkin and smashed it.

3. Which of the following is the best *closing sentence* for the paragraph above?

    A. We like making pumpkin pie.

    B. My mom bought a white pumpkin.

    C. One year, my dad stepped on a pumpkin and smashed it.

    D. Going to the pumpkin patch is fun.

To complete the assessment, complete the paragraph writing prompt on the following page.

ASSESSMENT

ASSESSMENT

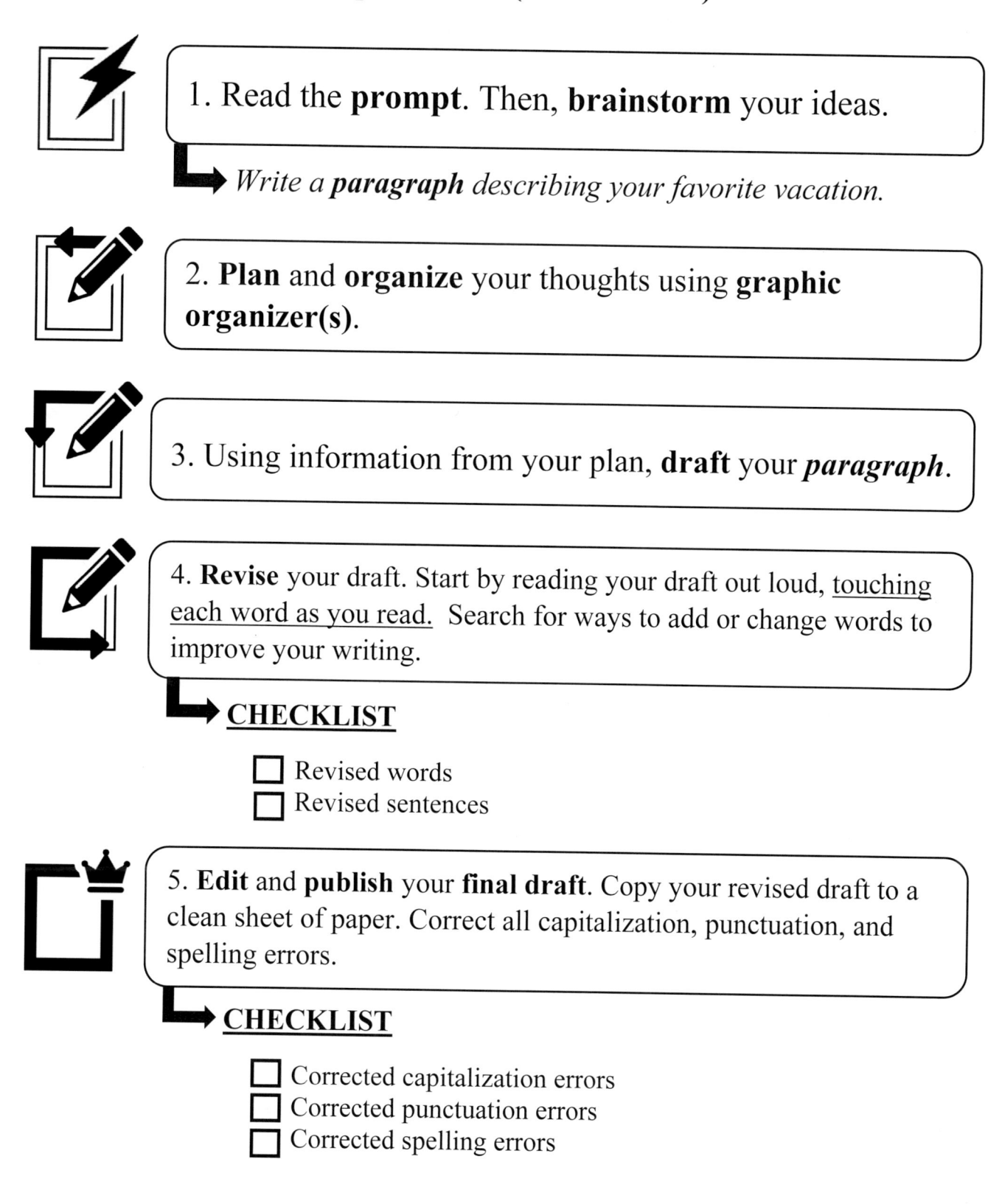

Assessment 16 – Paragraph Practice (Lessons 38-43)

1. Read the **prompt**. Then, **brainstorm** your ideas.

   *Write a **paragraph** describing your favorite vacation.*

2. **Plan** and **organize** your thoughts using **graphic organizer(s)**.

3. Using information from your plan, **draft** your *paragraph*.

4. **Revise** your draft. Start by reading your draft out loud, <u>touching each word as you read.</u> Search for ways to add or change words to improve your writing.

   CHECKLIST
   - ☐ Revised words
   - ☐ Revised sentences

5. **Edit** and **publish** your **final draft**. Copy your revised draft to a clean sheet of paper. Correct all capitalization, punctuation, and spelling errors.

   CHECKLIST
   - ☐ Corrected capitalization errors
   - ☐ Corrected punctuation errors
   - ☐ Corrected spelling errors

ASSESSMENT

Paragraph Practice Checklist

- I indented my opening sentence. ___/1
- I wrote an opening sentence. ___/1
- I wrote three or more body sentences. ___/1
- I stayed on topic. ___/1
- I wrote a closing sentence. ___/1
- I checked my spelling. ___/1
- I used capitalization correctly. ___/1
- I used punctuation correctly. ___/1
- My handwriting is neat, and my words are spaced correctly. ___/1

Remember, good writing takes practice!

Total Points: ___/9

ASSESSMENT

_____ / 8 points

Assessment 17 – Expository Writing (Lessons 44-53)

Circle the letter next to the correct answer

1. Expository writing…

    A. explains, describes, or informs.

    B. tries to convince a reader using facts and examples to support an opinion.

    C. describes someone or something using sensory details.

    D. is an imagined or make-believe story about a series of events.

2. In which step of the writing process do you plan your opening, body, and closing sentences?

    A. Brainstorm

    B. Organize

    C. Draft

    D. Revise

3. The parts of a personal letter are…

    A. pictures, jokes, drawings, stories.

    B. date, greeting, body, closing, and signature.

    C. questions, answers, ideas, opinions, and recipes.

    D. top, beginning, middle, end, and bottom.

4. Which topic would you write about for an expository paragraph?

    A. Your favorite movie and why you like it

    B. A dragon who can't fly

    C. Convincing your mom to buy a guinea pig

    D. Telling your brother why he should take you to the movies

To complete the assessment, complete <u>one</u> of the expository writing prompts on the following page.

ASSESSMENT

ASSESSMENT

Assessment 17 – Expository Writing (Lessons 44-53)

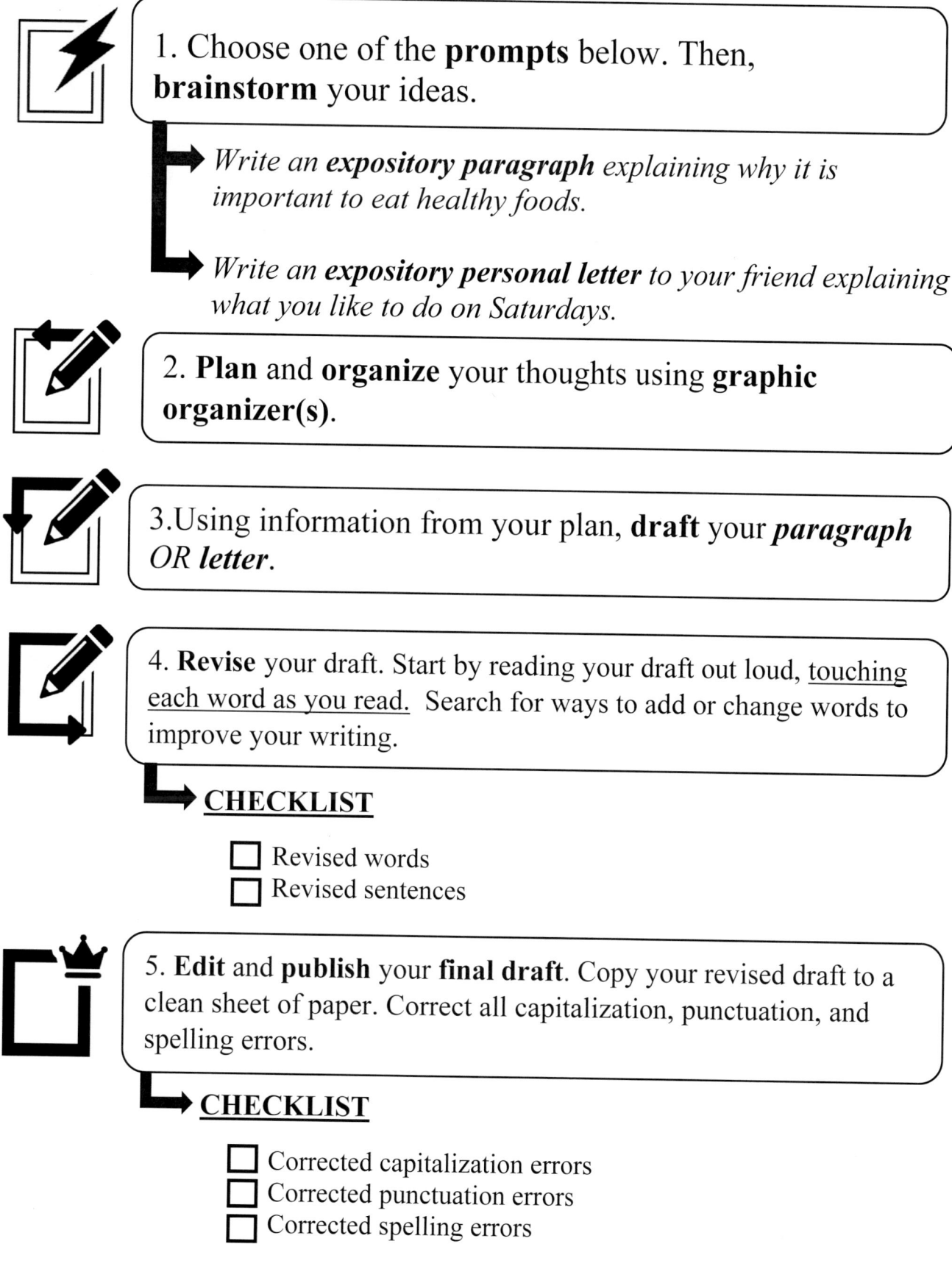

1. Choose one of the **prompts** below. Then, **brainstorm** your ideas.

    → *Write an **expository paragraph** explaining why it is important to eat healthy foods.*

    → *Write an **expository personal letter** to your friend explaining what you like to do on Saturdays.*

2. **Plan** and **organize** your thoughts using **graphic organizer(s)**.

3. Using information from your plan, **draft** your *paragraph* OR *letter*.

4. **Revise** your draft. Start by reading your draft out loud, <u>touching each word as you read.</u> Search for ways to add or change words to improve your writing.

    → **CHECKLIST**

    ☐ Revised words
    ☐ Revised sentences

5. **Edit** and **publish** your **final draft**. Copy your revised draft to a clean sheet of paper. Correct all capitalization, punctuation, and spelling errors.

    → **CHECKLIST**

    ☐ Corrected capitalization errors
    ☐ Corrected punctuation errors
    ☐ Corrected spelling errors

ASSESSMENT

Expository Paragraph Checklist

- I indented my opening sentence. ___/ 1

- I wrote an opening sentence. ___/ 1

- I wrote three or more body sentences. ___/ 1

- I stayed on topic. ___/ 1

- I wrote a closing sentence. ___/ 1

- I checked my spelling. ___/ 1

- I used capitalization correctly. ___/ 1

- I used punctuation correctly. ___/ 1

- My handwriting is neat, and my words are spaced correctly. ___/ 1

Remember, good writing takes practice!

Total Points: ___/9

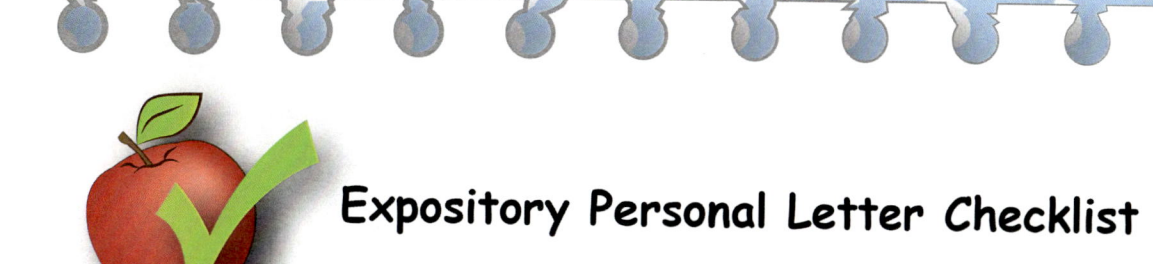

ASSESSMENT

Expository Personal Letter Checklist

- I indented my opening sentence. ___/1
- I wrote an opening sentence. ___/1
- I wrote three or more body sentences. ___/1
- I stayed on topic. ___/1
- I wrote a closing sentence. ___/1
- I checked my spelling. ___/1
- I used capitalization correctly. ___/1
- I used punctuation correctly. ___/1
- My handwriting is neat, and my words are spaced correctly. ___/1
- I included and correctly formatted all parts of a letter. ___/1
  - DATE • GREETING • CLOSING • SIGNATURE

Remember, good writing takes practice!

Total Points: ___/10

ASSESSMENT

ASSESSMENT

_____ / 8 points

Assessment 18 – Persuasive Writing (Lessons 54-63)

Circle the letter next to the correct answer.

1. Persuasive writing…

   A. explains, describes, or informs.

   B. tries to convince a reader using facts and examples to support an opinion.

   C. describes someone or something using sensory details.

   D. is an imagined or make-believe story about a series of events.

2. Which topic would you write about in a persuasive paragraph?

   A. What you did last Christmas with your grandparents

   B. Your plan for decorating your bedroom

   C. What you know about elephants

   D. Why people should not throw trash on the side of the road

3. The opening sentence of your persuasive paragraph should include _____.

   A. your persuasive opinion

   B. expository ideas

   C. sensory details

   D. a funny joke

4. Persuasive writing can try to convince someone to believe or not believe something or…

   A. to know more information about a topic.

   B. to do or not do something.

   C. to imagine a fantastic story.

   D. to understand new details.

To complete the assessment, complete <u>one</u> of the persuasive writing prompts on the following page.

ASSESSMENT

ASSESSMENT

Assessment 18 – Persuasive Writing (Lessons 54-63)

1. Choose one of the **prompts** below. Then, **brainstorm** your ideas.

> *Write a **persuasive paragraph** telling someone why they should read a certain book.*
>
> *Write a **persuasive personal letter** to your friend about what you both should do during summer vacation. Be sure to include all parts of a letter.*

2. **Plan** and **organize** your thoughts using **graphic organizer(s)**.

3. Using information from your plan, **draft** your *paragraph* OR *letter*.

4. **Revise** your draft. Start by reading your draft out loud, <u>touching each word as you read.</u> Search for ways to add or change words to improve your writing.

CHECKLIST

- ☐ Revised words
- ☐ Revised sentences

5. **Edit** and **publish** your **final draft**. Copy your revised draft to a clean sheet of paper. Correct all capitalization, punctuation, and spelling errors.

CHECKLIST

- ☐ Corrected capitalization errors
- ☐ Corrected punctuation errors
- ☐ Corrected spelling errors

ASSESSMENT

Persuasive Paragraph Checklist

I indented my opening sentence. ___/1

My opening sentence introduces my persuasive opinion. ___/1

I wrote three or more body sentences. ___/1

My body sentences include details that support my opinion. ___/1

I stayed on topic. ___/1

I wrote a closing sentence. ___/1

I checked my spelling. ___/1

I used capitalization correctly. ___/1

I used punctuation correctly. ___/1

My handwriting is neat, and my words are spaced correctly. ___/1

Remember, good writing takes practice!

Total Points: ___/ 10

ASSESSMENT

Persuasive Personal Letter Checklist

- I indented my opening sentence. ___/1
- My opening sentence introduces my persuasive opinion. ___/1
- I wrote three or more body sentences. ___/1
- My body sentences include details that support my persuasive opinion. ___/1
- I stayed on topic. ___/1
- I wrote a closing sentence. ___/1
- I checked my spelling ___/1
- I used capitalization correctly. ___/1
- I used punctuation correctly. ___/1
- My handwriting is neat, and my words are spaced correctly. ___/1
- I included and correctly formatted all parts of a letter. ___/1
  - DATE • GREETING • CLOSING • SIGNATURE

Remember, good writing takes practice!

Total Points: ___/11

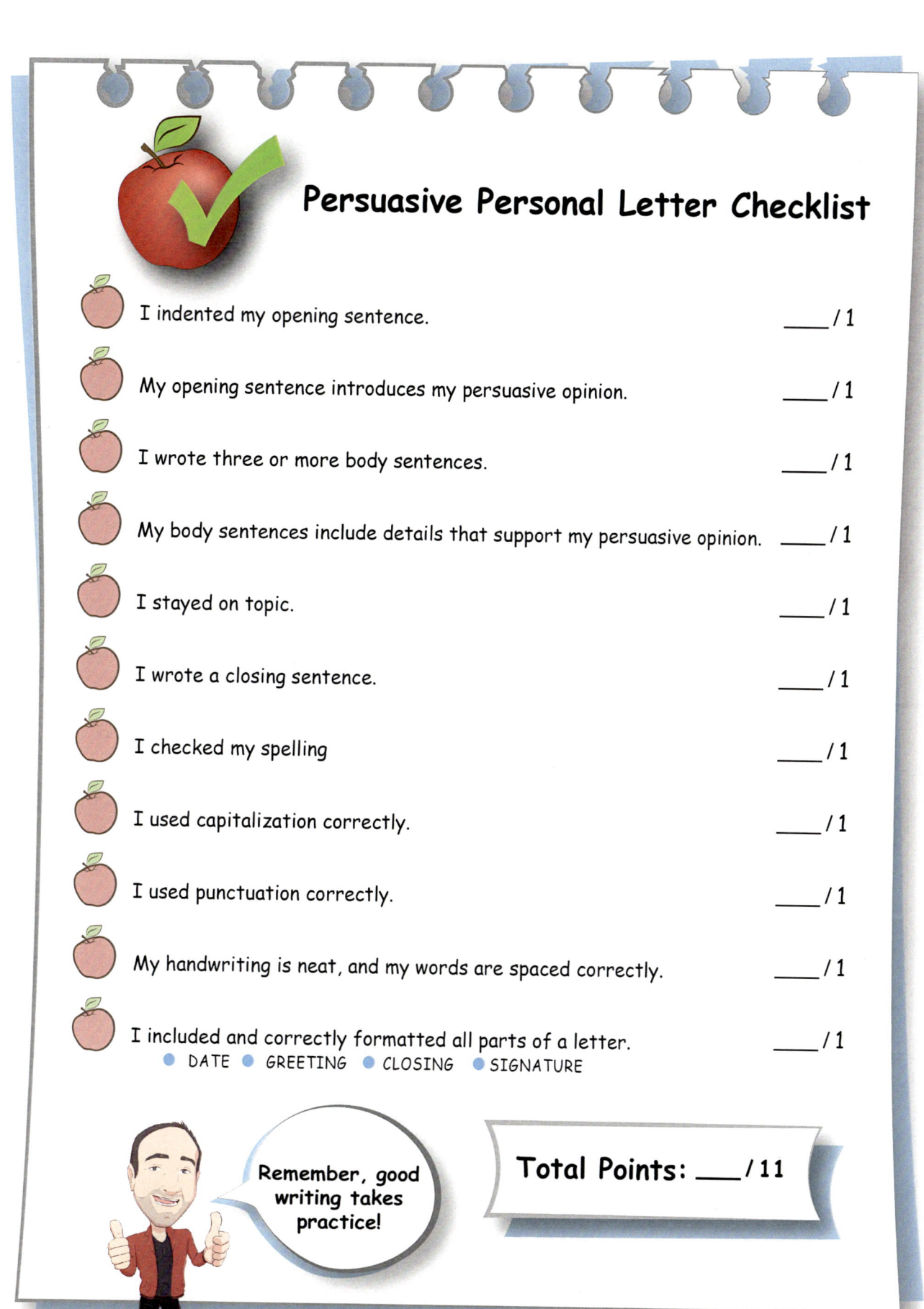

ASSESSMENT

ASSESSMENT

_____ / 8 points

Assessment 19 – Descriptive Writing (Lessons 64-73)
Circle the letter next to the correct answer.

1. Descriptive writing…

    A. explains, describes, or informs.

    B. tries to convince a reader using facts and examples to support an opinion.

    C. describes someone or something using sensory details.

    D. talks about types of bread.

2. Which of the following sentences contains *sensory details*?

    A. Chuck was bored.

    B. My brother liked the good soup.

    C. Did you do your homework?

    D. The fresh, sparkly snow was icy cold.

3. What are the five types of *physical senses*?

    A. sight, sound, taste, touch, smell

    B. big, small, high, low, inside

    C. colors, textures, music, feelings, thoughts

    D. red, yellow, blue, green, white

4. *Hook, events, climax,* and *closing* are all parts of a(n)…

    A. expository letter.

    B. persuasive paragraph.

    C. imaginative narrative.

    D. research project.

To complete the assessment, complete __one__ of the descriptive writing prompts on the following page.

ASSESSMENT

ASSESSMENT

ASSESSMENT

Assessment 19 – Descriptive Writing (Lessons 64-73)

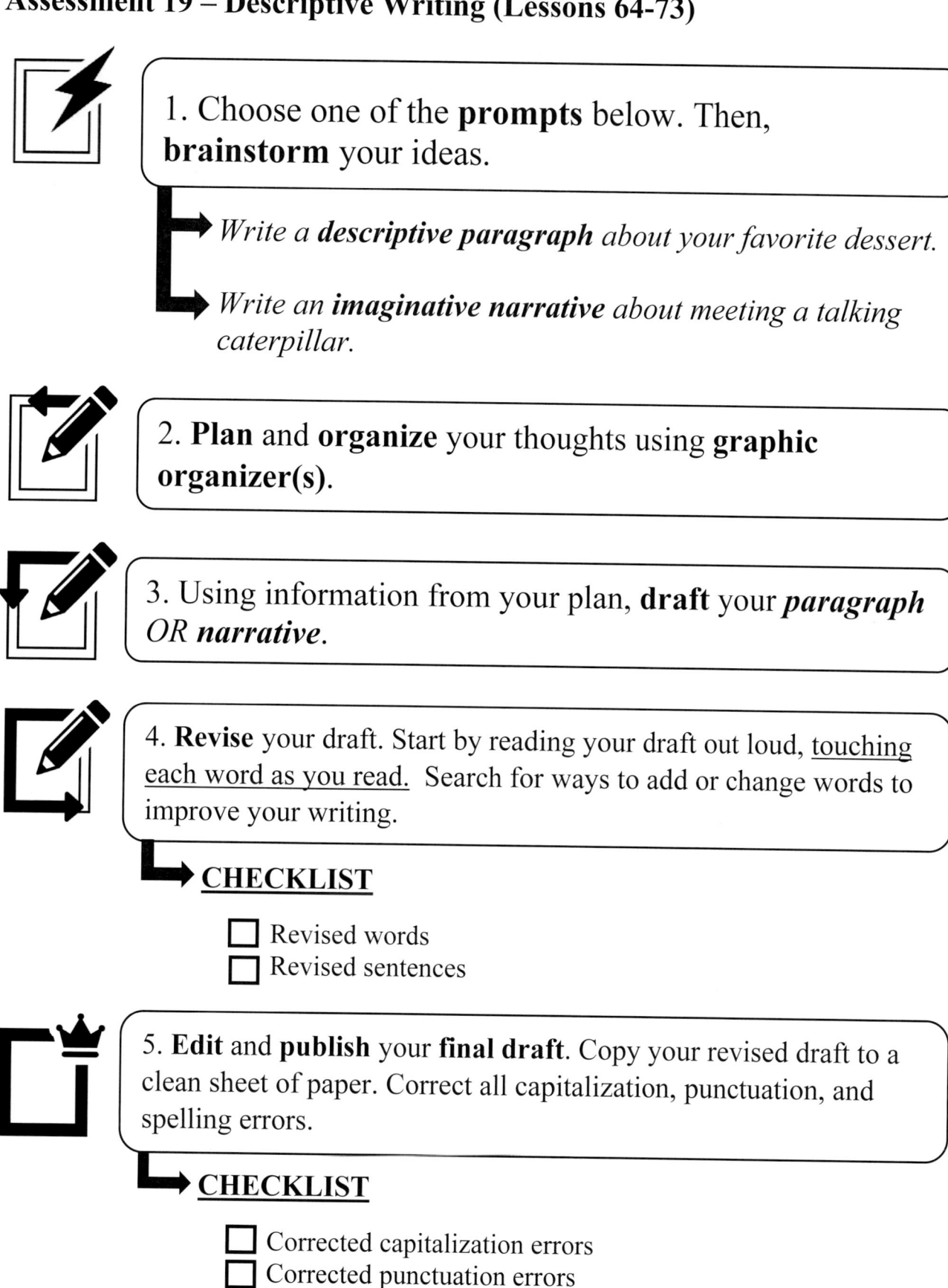

1. Choose one of the **prompts** below. Then, **brainstorm** your ideas.

> *Write a **descriptive paragraph** about your favorite dessert.*
>
> *Write an **imaginative narrative** about meeting a talking caterpillar.*

2. **Plan** and **organize** your thoughts using **graphic organizer(s)**.

3. Using information from your plan, **draft** your ***paragraph*** OR ***narrative***.

4. **Revise** your draft. Start by reading your draft out loud, <u>touching each word as you read.</u> Search for ways to add or change words to improve your writing.

CHECKLIST

☐ Revised words
☐ Revised sentences

5. **Edit** and **publish** your **final draft**. Copy your revised draft to a clean sheet of paper. Correct all capitalization, punctuation, and spelling errors.

CHECKLIST

☐ Corrected capitalization errors
☐ Corrected punctuation errors
☐ Corrected spelling errors

ASSESSMENT

Descriptive Paragraph Checklist

- I indented my opening sentence. ___/1
- I wrote an opening sentence. ___/1
- I wrote three or more body sentences. ___/1
- My body sentences include sensory details. ___/1
- I stayed on topic. ___/1
- I wrote a closing sentence. ___/1
- I checked my spelling. ___/1
- I used capitalization correctly. ___/1
- I used punctuation correctly. ___/1
- My handwriting is neat, and my words are spaced correctly. ___/1

Remember, good writing takes practice!

Total Points: ___/10

ASSESSMENT

Imaginative Narrative Checklist

- I indented my opening sentence. ___/1
- My opening sentence grabs the reader's attention. ___/1
- I wrote at least two events and a climax. ___/1
- My events are written in chronological order. ___/1
- I used at least three transitions. ___/1
- I used sensory details. ___/1
- I checked my spelling. ___/1
- I used capitalization correctly. ___/1
- I used punctuation correctly. ___/1
- My handwriting is neat, and my words are spaced correctly. ___/1

Remember, good writing takes practice!

Total Points: ___/10

ASSESSMENT

ASSESSMENT

_____ / 34 points

Unit 2 Comprehensive Assessment (Lessons 32-73)

Circle the letter next to the correct answer

1. _____ is <u>not</u> part of the writing process.

   A. Brainstorming

   B. Organizing

   C. Erasing

   D. Revising

2. What is the purpose of the *brainstorming* step of the writing process?

   A. To put ideas in order

   B. To plan with a graphic organizer

   C. To revise the work

   D. To choose a topic

3. What do you do in the *organize* step of the writing process?

   A. Publish your final draft

   B. Choose a topic

   C. Use a graphic organizer to help organize your ideas

   D. Use your plan to begin writing

4. In the writing process, _____ is when you use the ideas from your plan.

   A. drafting

   B. brainstorming

   C. editing

   D. revising

ASSESSMENT

5. What is the purpose of the *revision* step of the writing process?

    A. Improving your writing

    B. Publishing your final copy

    C. Planning what you will write

    D. Putting your ideas in order

6. A *final draft* is…

    A. the final copy with all corrections made.

    B. a list of ideas.

    C. a graphic organizer.

    D. a revision checklist.

Read the following paragraph:

Airplanes are amazing. They fly high in the sky. Many people can fit inside planes. The pilot sits in the front. We ate toast before flying on a plane. Airplanes are great.

7. Which sentence does *not* stay on topic in the paragraph above?

    A. They fly high in the sky.

    B. Many people can fit inside planes.

    C. The pilot sits in the front.

    D. We ate toast before flying on a plane.

8. What is the purpose of *expository writing*?

    A. to explain, describe, or inform

    B. to try to convince a reader using facts and examples to support an opinion

    C. to describe someone or something using sensory details

    D. to tell an imagined or make-believe story about a series of events

ASSESSMENT

9. What are the five parts of a *personal letter*?

   A. brainstorm, draft, organize, revise, final draft

   B. date, greeting, body, closing, and signature

   C. opening, beginning, middle, end, closing

   D. sight, sound, taste, touch, smell

10. Persuasive writing tries to…

    A. explain, describe, or inform.

    B. convince a reader using facts and examples to support an opinion.

    C. describe someone or something using sensory details.

    D. tell an imaginative story.

11. Descriptive writing tries to…

    A. explain, describe, or inform.

    B. convince a reader using facts and examples to support an opinion.

    C. describe someone or something using sensory details.

    D. explain how to use something.

12. A(n) _____ is an imagined or make-believe story about a series of events.

    A. personal letter

    B. expository paragraph

    C. persuasive letter

    D. imaginative narrative

13. The three parts of a paragraph are…

    A. details, ending, and conclusion.

    B. body, middle, and end.

    C. opening, body, and closing.

    D. beginning, details, and middle.

ASSESSMENT

14. Which of the following would be the topic of an expository letter?

    A. A new game you want to play

    B. Why your dad should buy you new shoes

    C. A made-up story about talking spiders

    D. Why your mom should take you to the movies

15. Which of the following would be the topic of a persuasive letter?

    A. A story about flying in a hot-air balloon

    B. Information about how to change a tire on a car

    C. Why your family should buy a pool

    D. What a homemade birthday cake tastes like

Read the following paragraph:

You should watch more shows about real life. Shows about real life help you learn more about other people. You can also learn how things are made and how things work. If you watch these kinds of shows, you will know more about the world. Watching shows about real life would be good for you.

16. What kind of writing is the paragraph above?

    A. Expository

    B. Descriptive

    C. Persuasive

    D. Imaginative Narrative

17. *Emma and Maddison wore big, fluffy hats made of soft, warm, grey wool.*

    Which of the following *best* describes this kind of writing?

    A. Descriptive

    B. Expository

    C. Imaginative

    D. Persuasive

Resources

Spelling Dictionary

Aa

about

again

already

always

animal

any

are

asked

across

almost

also

and

another

anyone

around

aunt

Spelling Dictionary

Bb

babies	baby
balloon	bear
beautiful	because
been	before
believe	black
blow	blue
bought	brother
brown	buy
by	

69

Spelling Dictionary

Cc

call
change
choose
Christmas
clothes
color
coming
cousin

can't
children
chose
climb
cold
come
could
cry

Dd

decide
different
doctor
doesn't
don't
drop

didn't
do
does
done
draw

Spelling Dictionary

Ee

early	earth
easy	eight
enough	even
ever	every
everything	except
excited	eye

Spelling Dictionary

Ff

family
favorite
finally
follow
found
fourth
friend

father
February
first
forty
four
Friday
from

Spelling Dictionary

Gg

get
give
good
grandpa
guess

gift
goes
grandma
great
guest

Hh

half	happened
have	hear
heard	heart
here	honey
hope	horse
hour	house

Spelling Dictionary

Ii

ice cream	if
I'll	insect
inside	instead
interesting	into
is	isn't
it	

Spelling Dictionary

Spelling Dictionary

Jj

January　　jealous

jiggle　　joke

jump　　just

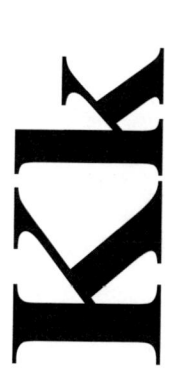

Spelling Dictionary

Kk

key
kind
knew
know

keyboard
king
knock

Spelling Dictionary

Ll

ladder	later
laugh	learn
let's	letter
light	like
listen	little
look	loose
lose	love

Mm

many	maybe
might	milk
minute	Monday
money	more
morning	mother
mouse	move
my	myself

Spelling Dictionary

Spelling Dictionary

Nn

neighbor	never
new	next
nice	night
nine	ninety
ninth	none
nothing	now
nurse	

Oo

obey	of
off	often
once	one
only	open
opposite	orange
our	

Pp

party — people

perfect — person

picture — piece

pink — please

point — practice

probably — purple

put

Spelling Dictionary

Qq

quack	quarter
queen	question
quick	quiet
quilt	quit
quiz	

Spelling Dictionary

Rr

read
really
remember
ring
rough

ready
reason
right
roar

Spelling Dictionary

Ss

safe	said
Saturday	says
school	should
sister	some
something	sometimes
special	Sunday
sure	surprise

Spelling Dictionary

Tt

the
there
they
thought
through
tickle
together
tonight
Tuesday

their
these
they're
threw
Thursday
today
tomorrow
tough
two

Uu

umbrella

until

upon

us

use

used

usual

usually

Spelling Dictionary

Spelling Dictionary

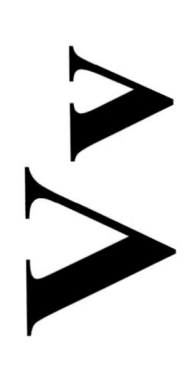

Vv

vacation	very
video	view
volume	voice
vowel	

Spelling Dictionary

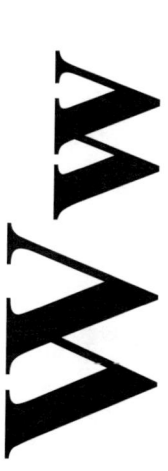

Ww

want
wear
Wednesday
went
what
where
who
won't
world
write

was
weather
weird
were
when
white
with
work
would

Spelling Dictionary

Xx

x-ray
xylophone

Yy

yellow
yesterday
you
your
you're

Zz

zebra
zero

RESOURCES
Sensory Word List

Sensory details are details that appeal to the reader's five physical senses: *sight, sound, touch, taste,* and *smell*. Use descriptive **nouns, adjectives,** and ***action verbs*** to add sensory details to your writing.

SENSORY WORDS

SIGHT

bright	hazy		
colorful	light		
dark	misty		
dim	shadowy		
faded	spotted		
faint	sparkling		
foggy	striped		
glistening	swaying		
gloomy	twisted		

SOUND

boom	rustle
buzz	roar
cheer	scream
clang	squeal
crash	thud
explode	thump
giggle	wheeze
gurgling	whimper
howl	yelp

TOUCH

bristly	metallic
bumpy	moist
chilly	silky
cold	springy
dusty	sticky
fuzzy	stiff
gooey	sweaty
greasy	waxy
hairy	wiry

TASTE AND SMELL

bitter	old
bland	peppery
creamy	ripe
flavorful	rotten
fresh	smoky
juicy	sour
moldy	sugary
musty	tasty
odor	whiff

RESOURCES

Action Verb List

Using *descriptive action verbs* makes your writing interesting to the reader. Some *action verbs* do a better job than others at showing the reader the action of the sentence. The best *action verbs* show the reader the action, not just tell the reader the action.

ACTION VERBS

accept	effect	obey	support
admire	enjoy	ooze	taught
advise	exit	organize	tease
amble	explore	peek	test
assemble	float	predict	thrash
bellow	focus	produce	update
boast	gasp	pursue	utilize
bolt	glide	qualify	vault
cast	gush	race	vent
channel	howl	reduce	visit
cherish	hurl	repair	wait
collect	ignite	respond	wander
compose	impress	search	yearn
craft	journey	shape	yell
dawdle	listen	sigh	yodel
describe	loom	sink	zap

RESOURCES

Descriptive Adjective Word List

When communicating in written language, it is important to be able to express your ideas effectively. *Word choice* is a key aspect of effective communication. The following word lists are alternatives to overused words.

To improve communication, replace ineffective words with powerful words.

BAD
awful	hurtful
careless	harmful
crummy	ill
terrible	poor
lousy	dreadful

HAPPY
carefree	jolly
cheerful	joyful
content	pleased
delighted	sunny
thrilled	glad

PRETTY
attractive	charming
beautiful	elegant
delightful	fair
charming	lovely
graceful	handsome

GOOD
excellent	fantastic
wonderful	great
dandy	healthy
delightful	helpful
proper	friendly

RESOURCES

Descriptive Action Verb Word List

When communicating in written language, it is important to be able to express your ideas effectively. ***Word choice*** is a key aspect of effective communication. The following word lists are alternatives to overused words.

To improve communication, replace ineffective words with powerful words.

WENT
traveled	walked
flew	escaped
exited	journeyed
drove	visited
wandered	sailed

SAID
mentioned	replied
repeated	claimed
stated	declared
shouted	guessed
answered	revealed

RAN
dashed	hurried
jogged	bolted
rushed	scampered
raced	scrambled
sped	hustled

HAD
held	possessed
carried	included
owned	gained
enjoyed	picked up
accepted	collected

RESOURCES

Expository Paragraph
Graphic Organizer

Write ideas for the beginning of your paragraph. Write what your topic is.

Opening

Write ideas for the middle of your paragraph. Write details about your topic.

Detail

Detail

Detail

Write ideas for the end of your paragraph. Close your topic.

Closing

RESOURCES

Expository Paragraph Checklist

- I indented my opening sentence. ___/1
- I wrote an opening sentence. ___/1
- I wrote three or more body sentences. ___/1
- I stayed on topic. ___/1
- I wrote a closing sentence. ___/1
- I checked my spelling. ___/1
- I used capitalization correctly. ___/1
- I used punctuation correctly. ___/1
- My handwriting is neat, and my words are spaced correctly. ___/1

Remember, good writing takes practice!

Total Points: ___/9

Persuasive Paragraph Graphic Organizer

Write ideas for the beginning of your paragraph. Write what your topic is.

Opening

Write ideas for the middle of your paragraph. Write details about your topic.

Detail

Detail

Detail

Write ideas for the end of your paragraph. Close your topic.

Closing

RESOURCES

Persuasive Paragraph Checklist

I indented my opening sentence. ___/ 1

My opening sentence introduces my persuasive opinion. ___/ 1

I wrote three or more body sentences. ___/ 1

My body sentences include details that support my opinion. ___/ 1

I stayed on topic. ___/ 1

I wrote a closing sentence. ___/ 1

I checked my spelling. ___/ 1

I used capitalization correctly. ___/ 1

I used punctuation correctly. ___/ 1

My handwriting is neat, and my words are spaced correctly. ___/ 1

Remember, good writing takes practice!

Total Points: ___/ 10

**Descriptive Paragraph
Graphic Organizer**

- Write ideas for the beginning of your paragraph. Write what your topic is.

Opening

- Write ideas for the middle of your paragraph. Write details about your topic.

Detail

Detail

Detail

- Write ideas for the end of your paragraph. Close your topic.

Closing

RESOURCES

Descriptive Paragraph Checklist

I indented my opening sentence. ___ / 1

I wrote an opening sentence. ___ / 1

I wrote three or more body sentences. ___ / 1

My body sentences include sensory details. ___ / 1

I stayed on topic. ___ / 1

I wrote a closing sentence. ___ / 1

I checked my spelling. ___ / 1

I used capitalization correctly. ___ / 1

I used punctuation correctly. ___ / 1

My handwriting is neat, and my words are spaced correctly. ___ / 1

Remember, good writing takes practice!

Total Points: ___ / 10

RESOURCES

Expository Personal Letter
Graphic Organizer

💡 Write ideas for the beginning of your letter. Write what your topic is.

Opening

💡 Write ideas for the middle of your letter. Write details about your topic.

Detail

Detail

Detail

💡 Write ideas for the end of your letter. Close your topic.

Closing

RESOURCES

Expository Personal Letter Checklist

I indented my opening sentence. ___/1

I wrote an opening sentence. ___/1

I wrote three or more body sentences. ___/1

I stayed on topic. ___/1

I wrote a closing sentence. ___/1

I checked my spelling. ___/1

I used capitalization correctly. ___/1

I used punctuation correctly. ___/1

My handwriting is neat, and my words are spaced correctly. ___/1

I included and correctly formatted all parts of a letter. ___/1
• DATE • GREETING • CLOSING • SIGNATURE

Remember, good writing takes practice!

Total Points: ___/10

RESOURCES

Persuasive Personal Letter Graphic Organizer

💡 Write ideas for the beginning of your letter. Write what your topic is.

Opening

💡 Write ideas for the middle of your letter. Write details about your topic.

Detail

Detail

Detail

💡 Write ideas for the end of your letter. Close your topic.

Closing

RESOURCES

Persuasive Personal Letter Checklist

I indented my opening sentence. ___/1

My opening sentence introduces my persuasive opinion. ___/1

I wrote three or more body sentences. ___/1

My body sentences include details that support my persuasive opinion. ___/1

I stayed on topic. ___/1

I wrote a closing sentence. ___/1

I checked my spelling ___/1

I used capitalization correctly. ___/1

I used punctuation correctly. ___/1

My handwriting is neat, and my words are spaced correctly. ___/1

I included and correctly formatted all parts of a letter. ___/1
• DATE • GREETING • CLOSING • SIGNATURE

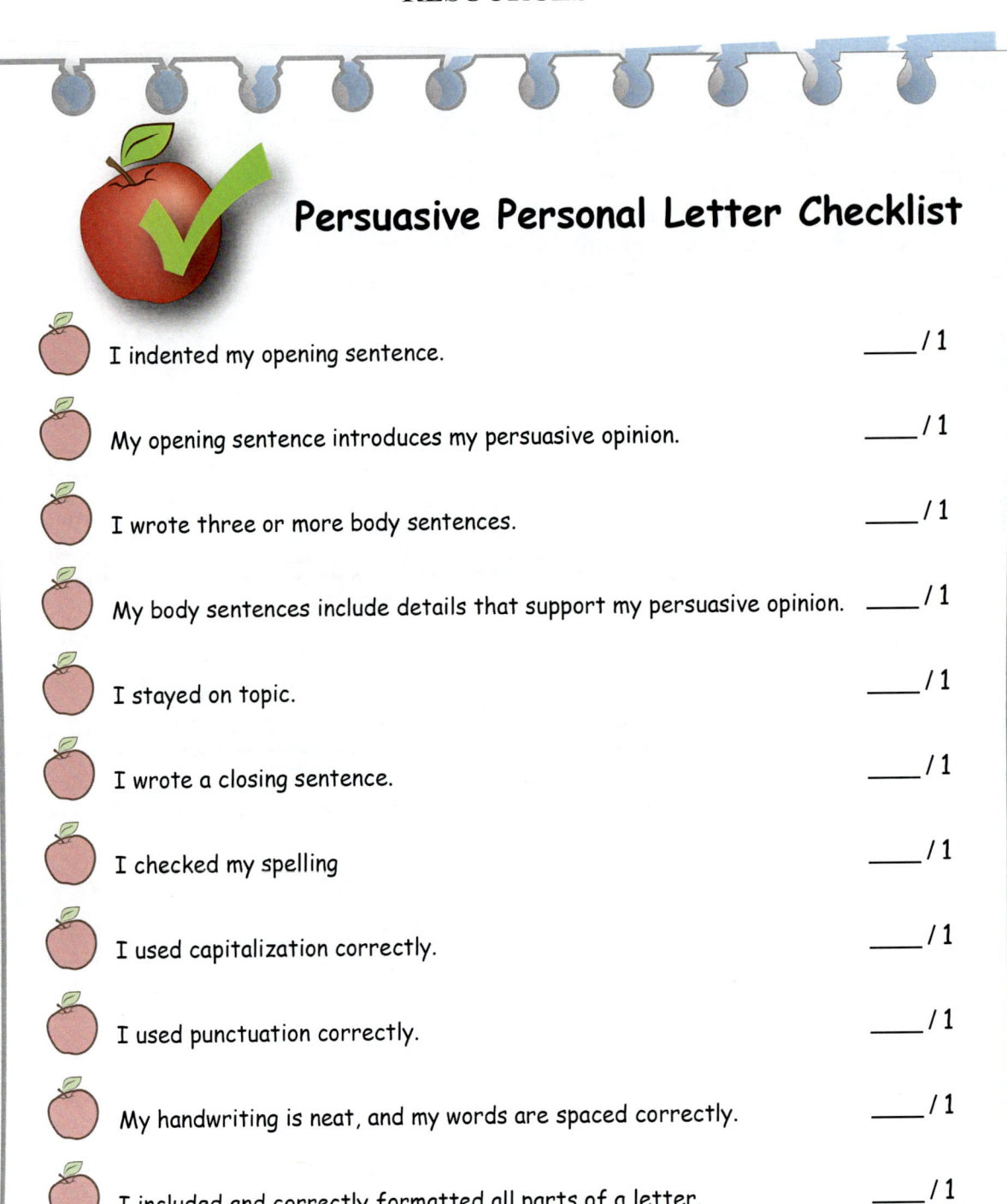

Remember, good writing takes practice!

Total Points: ___/11

RESOURCES

Imaginative Narrative Graphic Organizer

- Hook
- Event
- Event
- Climax
- Problem
- Solution
- Closing

106

RESOURCES

Imaginative Narrative Checklist

- I indented my opening sentence. ___/1
- My opening sentence grabs the reader's attention. ___/1
- I wrote at least two events and a climax. ___/1
- My events are written in chronological order. ___/1
- I used at least three transitions. ___/1
- I used sensory details. ___/1
- I checked my spelling. ___/1
- I used capitalization correctly. ___/1
- I used punctuation correctly. ___/1
- My handwriting is neat, and my words are spaced correctly. ___/1

Remember, good writing takes practice!

Total Points: ___/10

Supplemental Words Levels 1-3

Level 1 Word List - Lesson 9
Words to Begin a Sentence

the	I	a	an	my
it	his	we	he	she
this	her	they	that	(a name)

Level 1 Word List - Lesson 10
Question Words

is	are	do	did
does	can	how	what
when	where	why	who
whom			

Words to Use Instead of…Said

asked	called	stated
cried	demanded	exclaimed
shouted	whispered	replied
remarked		

Words to Use Instead of…Went

ran	rode	walked	crept
drove	biked	tiptoed	hiked
hopped	jumped	jogged	wandered
flew	climbed	strolled	

Words to Use Instead of…Like

love	adore	admire
prefer	care for	enjoy
treasure	favor	appreciate

RESOURCES

Supplemental Words Levels 1-3

Words to Use Instead of...Good

great   excellent   marvelous   superior
wonderful   fantastic   splendid   superb
awesome   terrific   stupendous
grand   extraordinary   amazing

Words to Use Instead of...Bad

terrible   crummy   awful   lousy
rough   rotten   gross   nasty
dreadful   unpleasant   unfortunate   vile
evil   wicked   despicable

Words to Use Instead of...Big

large   huge   giant
ginormous   gigantic   immense
tremendous   colossal   massive
jumbo   monster

Words to Use Instead of...Small

little   tiny   teeny   teensy
short   baby   mini   miniature
puny   wee

Words to Use Instead of...Happy

glad   merry   jolly
cheerful   joyful   gleeful
overjoyed   thrilled   pleased
tickled   jubilant

RESOURCES

Supplemental Words Levels 1-3

Words to Use Instead of...Sad
upset   discouraged   troubled   gloomy
disturbed   unhappy   disappointed   down
hopeless   sorrowful   miserable

Words to Use Instead of...Nice
kind   thoughtful   kindly   fair
gracious   pleasant   sweet   charming
agreeable   good   delightful
considerate   lovely

Words to Use Instead of...Pretty
cute   beautiful   handsome   lovely
fair   attractive   stunning   nice
fine   good-looking   glamorous   neat
darling   elegant

Words to Use Instead of...Fast
quick   speedy   nimble   flying
swift   rapid   hasty   snappy
racing   dashing

Words to Use Instead of...Funny
comical   hilarious   ludicrous   ridiculous
playful   humorous   amusing   hysterical
jolly   silly   absurd   entertaining   laughable

Words to Use Instead of...Saw
spied   noticed   observed
noted   sighted   looked(at)
spotted   viewed   perceived

RESOURCES

Supplemental Words Levels 1-3

Level 1 Word List - Lesson 22
Colors

red   blue   yellow   green

orange   purple   pink   brown

black   white   gray

Animals
Level 1 Word List - Lesson 29
Pets

dog   tarantula   gerbil
hamster   frog   mouse
bird   rabbit   fish
snake   lizard   turtle
guinea pig   cat   hermit crab

Animals
Level 1 Word List - Lesson 29
Farm Animals

pig   horse   mule

donkey   goat   sheep   chicken

cow   turkey   duck   goose   rabbit

RESOURCES

Supplemental Words Levels 1-3

I Feel...

happy	nervous	bored	disgusted	lonely
sick	annoyed	hungry	frightened	
silly	ecstatic	sleepy	disappointed	
shy	shocked	scared	surprised	
proud	ashamed	excited	confused	
sad	confident	afraid	overwhelmed	
angry	jealous	guilty	embarrassed	

Transportation Words

hot air balloon	train	submarine	RV
four-wheeler	boat	helicopter	van
ambulance	canoe	fire engine	taxi
motorcycle	horse	police car	bus
bicycle	subway	sailboat	SUV
car	airplane	truck	tractor	wagon

Places to Go (Common Nouns)

home	school	zoo	restaurant
store	park	hospital	church
vacation	beach	gym	post office
game	bank	theater	mall

Level 2 Word List - Lesson 35
Transition Words (Order)

first second third
before after next
then finally following
later previously

RESOURCES

Supplemental Words Levels 1-3

Level 2 Word List - Lesson 12

Pronouns

I	you	he
it	they	we
him	her	us
them	me	she

Adjectives (Describing Words) Level 2 Word List - Lesson 13

Color
yellow	blue	green
orange	pink	gray
black	white	brown
	red	purple

Size
big	huge	large
giant	little	tiny
small	thin	thick
tall	short	long

Shape
square	flat	narrow
broad	curved	crooked
round	wide	straight	hollow

Taste
sweet	bitter	spicy
sour	bland	fruity
tangy	yummy	delicious
tasty		

RESOURCES

Supplemental Words Levels 1-3

Irregular Verbs (Level 2, Lesson 16)
Irregular Verbs do **not** follow the same tense pattern as other verbs.

Present Tense
say	run
tell	see
go	ride
win	sing
make	sleep
draw	do
meet	eat
come	fly
take	get
find	

Past Tense
said	ran
told	saw
went	rode
won	sang
made	slept
drew	did
met	ate
came	flew
took	got
found	

Linking Verbs (Level 2, Lesson 17)
A **linking verb** is a verb that connects the subject to a word or phrase in the predicate. It helps describe a subject instead of telling what the subject does.

Present Tense
- am
- are
- is

Past Tense
- was
- were
- was

RESOURCES

Supplemental Words Levels 1-3

Common and Proper Nouns (Level 3, Lesson 8)
A **common noun** is a word that is **any** person, place, thing, or idea. A **proper noun** is a word that is a **specific** person, place, thing, or idea, including titles.

Common Noun
- school
- country
- woman   boy
- store   dog
- restaurant   state
- city/town

Proper Noun
- Fairview Elementary
- United States of America
- Mrs. Jones   Mark Smith
- Walmart   Spot
- McDonalds   Texas
- Chicago

Adverbs (Level 3, Lesson 20)
An **adverb** tells how the subject is doing an action, such as:

How?
cheerfully carefully softly politely quickly quietly sadly
happily suddenly easily loudly silently closely well
badly slowly fast

How Much?
frequently enormously entirely quite
extremely very fairly almost too

How Often?
every day never never usually normally sometimes
always once often rarely seldom frequently

When?
before then now after early yesterday
already soon later since today tonight

Where?
away near here home outside everywhere
inside there far below behind

RESOURCES

Supplemental Words Levels 1-3

Onomatopoeia Words

Words that sound like the objects they name or the sounds those objects make.

Onomatopoeia Words

boom	crunch	whoosh	crash	pop
hiss	bzzz	oink	moo	ribbit
quack	woof	splash	swish	slurp
glug	boink	clank	achoo	snip
zing	rip	zip	pow	ding dong
tick tock	eek	whee	crack	vroom

RESOURCES

Assessment Answer Key

ASSESSMENT ANSWER KEY

Essentials in Writing Level 3 Assessment Answer Key

Unit One: Assessment Answer Key

Assessment 1 – Complete Subjects, Simple Subjects, Complete Predicates, & Simple Predicates (Lessons 2-5)
A. Complete the sentence with your own *simple subject*.
Answers may vary.
1. Casey dove into the water.
2. Geese flew across the sky.
3. Daniel likes pink lemonade.
4. Brownies smell delicious.
5. Gary rode a camel.
6. Rachel made s'mores.

B. Complete the sentence with your own *simple predicate*.
Answers may vary.
1. Her friend ran.
2. The tree fell.
3. The ball bounced.
4. My grandma baked.
5. The snake slithered.
6. Their pets sleep.

C. Complete each sentence with a *subject* or a *predicate*.
Answers may vary.
Layla had a birthday party. Her friends and family attended. They ate cake and ice cream. At the party, she opened presents. Layla received many gifts. Everyone had fun.

D. Circle the *simple subject* and underline the *simple predicate* in each sentence.
1. My {family} hosted a barbeque.
2. {Mom} grilled the hamburgers and hotdogs.
3. {Dad} made coleslaw and baked beans.
4. {Grandma} made homemade ice cream.
5. My {cousins and I} played games together.
6. {We} watched the fireworks.
7. The {fireworks} looked dazzling.
8. {Everyone} left late at night.
9. {I} dreamed about fireworks.
10. The {barbeque} was a fun event.

E. Circle the *complete subject* in each sentence.
1. {The boy in the blue shirt} shared his cookie.
2. {Dad} went to the store today.
3. {The man in the suit} opened the door for us.
4. {The orange kitten} hides under the bed.
5. {The woman in the red gown} spilled her drink.
6. {All the chipmunks} scampered away.
7. {That chubby puppy} is very cuddly.
8. {Martin} walked three miles.

F. Underline the *complete predicate* in each sentence.
1. Desiree wrote a story about talking ladybugs.
2. We danced in the rain.
3. I dreamed about a scary monster.
4. Laura rode on the big roller coaster.
5. The dog knows many tricks.
6. I watched a movie about dinosaurs.
7. Shyla planted trees for a school project.
8. Our family looked at the Christmas lights.

Assessment 2 – Complete and Incomplete Sentences, & Types of Sentences and Punctuation Marks (Lessons 6-7)
A. The following sentences are missing either a subject or a predicate. Complete each sentence with a subject or a predicate.
Answers may vary.
1. The teacher laughed loudly.
2. The dentist looked at the patient's teeth.
3. The author published a book.
4. Danny played the guitar.
5. Flora juggled at the talent show.
6. Our family ate homemade pizzas every Saturday night.
7. Dalton lifts heavy weights.

B. Write whether each sentence is *declarative*, *interrogative*, *exclamatory*, or *imperative*.
1. Interrogative
2. Exclamatory
3. Declarative
4. Imperative
5. Interrogative
6. Imperative
7. Declarative
8. Imperative
9. Exclamatory
10. Imperative

C. Underline the *complete sentences* and circle the *incomplete sentences* below.
1. I took the trash out.
2. The snow fell outside.
3. {Held the baby.}
4. {The broken cup.}
5. We packed for vacation.
6. {The cupcake.}
7. Her lizard eats grasshoppers.
8. {Their puppy.}

D. The sentences have mistakes in punctuation. Rewrite the sentence with correct punctuation.
1. Brush your teeth! OR .
2. Are you ready?
3. Let's play outside! OR .
4. Did you do the dishes?
5. Eat your vegetables! OR .

Assessment 3 – Common and Proper Nouns, & Singular and Plural Nouns (Lessons 8-9)
A. Circle each *proper noun*.
1. {Michael Jackson} was a pop star.
2. He was born in {Gary}, {Indiana}, in {August}.
3. {Michael Jackson} was part of a band called the {Jackson 5}.
4. He is known as the {King of Pop}.
5. {Michael} invented dance moves.

B. Underline each *common noun*.
1. Rose and I walked to the park.
2. We swung on the swings and went down the slide.
3. I brought granola bars for a snack.
4. I gave Rose one granola bar.
5. Evan walked into the park.

C. Fill in the blank with your own *proper noun*.
Answers may vary.
1. We flew to Montana for vacation. (*Place*)
2. I have a friend named Petey. (*Person*)
3. Stephanie is my cousin. (*Person*)
4. Australia is a country. (*Place*)
5. Abraham Lincoln was a president. (*Person*)

D. Fill in the blank with your own *common noun*.
1. The cowboy walked into the building. (*Person*)
2. I lost my backpack. (*Thing*)
3. Our family went to the zoo. (*Place*)

E. Underline the *common nouns* and circle the *proper nouns*.
1. tiger
2. {Betsy Ross}
3. rose
6. galaxy
7. {Brazil}
8. happiness
11. {Martin Luther King}
12. {American Music Award}
13. {New York}

ASSESSMENT ANSWER KEY

4. <u>medicine</u>
5. {Lucy Ball}
9. {Rebekah}
10. {California}
14. <u>notebook</u>
15. <u>yellow</u>

F. Underline each *common noun* and circle each *proper noun* in the paragraph.
   {Harry} made a new <u>friend</u> named {Charlie}. They have <u>class</u> with {Mrs. Robinson}. They met at <u>lunch</u>. {Harry} and {Charlie} had <u>sandwiches</u> and <u>chips</u>. They ate at the same <u>table</u>. {Harry} and {Charlie} played at <u>recess</u>. They climbed the <u>monkey bars</u> and slid down the <u>slide</u>. They played <u>tag</u> with {Donte.} {Harry} and {Charlie} are glad they are <u>friends</u>.

G. Underline the *singular nouns* and circle the *plural nouns* below.
1. The <u>teacher</u> likes her {students}.
2. There are muddy {footprints} all over the <u>floor</u>.
3. <u>Jenna</u> runs fast through the <u>forest</u>.
4. The {mountains} have huge {trees}.
5. <u>Trey</u> washes the {dishes} in the <u>sink</u>.

H. Fill in the blank with the *plural* of the indicated noun.
1. The children play in the backyard. (*child*)
2. The women laughed and told stories. (*woman*)
3. My friends and I sat at the front row of the concert! (*friend*)
4. The clouds look like a dinosaur in the sky. (*cloud*)
5. The repairman fixed the broken lights. (*light*)
6. My grandma baked a lot of cookies. (*cookie*)

Assessment 4 – Pronouns and Antecedents (Lesson 10)
A. Underline the *pronouns*.
1. Ariana caught the baseball. <u>She</u> is good at baseball.
2. Ryan performed a dance. <u>He</u> is graceful.
3. Liz shared <u>her</u> cookie with <u>me</u>. <u>I</u> was so happy!
4. Luke went on vacation to Canada. <u>He</u> told <u>us</u> all about <u>it</u>.

B. Circle the *antecedents*.
1. Our {family} put up the {Christmas tree}. We think it is pretty!
2. {Josephine} has a {test} tomorrow. She has to study hard for it.
3. The {cat} hissed at the dog. The dog ran away from it.
4. The {watch} broke. The watchmaker will fix it.

C. Rewrite the sentences and replace the underlined nouns with the correct pronouns.
1. Tammy told Steve that <u>his</u> cherry pie was the best she ever had.
2. Zara stayed up until midnight writing <u>her</u> paper.
3. The dog likes playing with the <u>his</u> **OR** <u>her</u> **OR** <u>its</u> toys.
4. Maria has to do <u>her</u> chores before going to bed.

D. Underline the *pronouns* and circle the *antecedents* in the paragraph below.
   {Jacob and Josiah} are twins! <u>They</u> both enjoy {dancing}. <u>They</u> are good at <u>it</u>! {Jacob} likes to dance ballet. {Josiah} likes to dance hip hop. <u>They</u> go to a dance studio almost every day. The {teachers} think <u>they</u> are talented. <u>They</u> want {Jacob and Josiah} want to go to dance school someday. {Jacob and Josiah} are excited for the future!

Assessment 5 – Singular Possessive Nouns, Plural Possessive Nouns, & More Plural Possessive Nouns (Lessons 11-13)
A. Use *singular possessive nouns* to shorten the phrases.
1. the pencil's eraser
2. the shirt's sleeve
3. the shoe's sole
4. the bird's feather

B. Use *plural possessive nouns* to shorten the phrases.
1. the families' presents
2. the kids' candy
3. the men's songs
4. the bees' honey

C. Combine the sentences using a *singular possessive noun*.
1. Drake's plaid shirt looked nice.
2. Danae's restaurant was busy.

D. Combine the sentences using a *plural possessive noun*.
1. The shelves' books fell.
2. The seamstresses' dresses were pretty.

Assessment 6 – Adjectives (Lesson 14)
A. Underline the *adjectives* in these sentences.
1. The <u>strong</u> wind whipped my hair.
2. The <u>calm</u> cats purred on my lap.
3. Mom flipped the <u>burnt</u> pancakes in the pan.
4. The <u>delicious</u> ice cream cone dripped on my arm.
5. We drove past the <u>bright</u> lights of the <u>big</u> city.
7. The <u>fluffy</u> pillows lie on the <u>soft</u> bed.
8. Dad put sunscreen on my <u>pale</u> skin.
9. The <u>nervous</u> speaker walked to the stage.
10. My <u>silly</u> uncle told a lot of <u>funny</u> jokes.

B. Complete each sentence with an *adjective*.
Answers may vary.
1. The sweater feels fuzzy.
2. I thought the book was very interesting.
3. Mom's lotion smells lovely.
4. The angry bull ran at the man.
5. The beautiful plate shattered into pieces.
6. The patient teacher taught the students math.
7. I held the cute hamster.

C. Underline the *adjectives* in the paragraph below.
   Vanessa plants <u>tiny</u> seeds in the <u>brown</u> soil. She works expertly in her <u>vegetable</u> garden. Vanessa grows <u>purple</u> eggplants, <u>green</u> cucumbers, and <u>yellow</u> squash. With the <u>fresh</u> vegetables, she makes <u>delicious</u> meals. Vanessa and her friends have a <u>great</u> time thinking of <u>new</u> recipes to use. She loves working in her garden and making <u>different</u> kinds of foods to eat and share.

Assessment 7 – Action Verbs; Present, Past, and Future Tense Action Verbs; Irregular Action Verbs; Linking Verbs; & Present, Past, and Future Tense Linking Verbs (Lessons 15-19)
A. Underline each *action verb*.
1. A friendly dog <u>belonged</u> to a little girl.
2. The girl <u>named</u> the dog Bolt.
3. Then, she <u>lost</u> Bolt on a rainy day.
4. However, she <u>found</u> her favorite puppy at the park.

B. Complete each sentence with an *action verb*.
Answers may vary.
1. The horse <u>ran</u> in the field.
2. Grandma <u>knit</u> a sweater for Grandpa.
3. The baby <u>slept</u> during the whole trip.
4. Uncle Albert <u>told</u> a funny story.

C. Write whether the underlined verbs are in the *present tense* or in the *past tense*.
1. Present
2. Present
3. Past
4. Past

D. Rewrite the sentences and change the *present tense* verbs to *past tense* verbs.
1. Angelica dropped her toy in the bucket.
2. Snow fell in winter.

E. Rewrite the sentences and change the *past tense* verbs to *present tense* verbs.
1. The punch will spill on the floor.
2. The couple will hold hands.

F. Underline each *linking verb*.
1. I <u>am</u> excited for the show!
2. This shirt <u>is</u> my lucky shirt.
3. Andrea <u>was</u> sick yesterday.
4. We <u>are</u> happy because it <u>is</u> the last day of school.
5. Jimmy and Matt <u>were</u> nervous for the test.

ASSESSMENT ANSWER KEY

G. Write whether the underlined linking verbs are in the *past,* *present,* **or** *future tense.*
1. Present
2. Future
3. Past

H. Rewrite the sentences to change the *present tense* **linking verbs to** *past tense* **linking verbs.**
1. Carol was a great singer.
2. Mom and Dad were in the garage.

I. Rewrite the sentences to change the *present tense* **linking verbs to** *future tense* **linking verbs.**
1. My turtle will be in the swimming pool.
2. I will be a space explorer.

Assessment 8 – Adverbs That Modify Verbs (Lesson 20)
A. Complete each sentence with your own *adverb.*
Answers may vary.
1. Melody quickly swam to the other side of the pool.
2. The zoo animals quietly slept at the end of the day.
3. The doctor kindly checked the patient.
4. My sister carefully finished her homework.
5. A little squirrel slowly came out of its hiding spot.

B. Underline each *adverb* **in the sentences.**
1. George nervously walked up onto the stage.
2. The snow softly fell to the ground.
3. Her book landed loudly after she dropped it.
4. Turtles don't always walk slowly.
5. My brother rarely cleans his room.
6. Carly did well on her test last Tuesday.

C. Underline each *adverb* **in the paragraph.**
Reindeer live in Alaska. Some people call them caribou. Some days, they playfully run around with each other. Reindeer eat grass daily. They can safely be in the snow all day. This is because they are completely covered with thick, warm fur. Their noses quickly warm up the air they breathe before it gets to their lungs. Reindeer are interesting animals!

D. Complete the paragraph with your own *adverbs.*
Answers may vary.
Josie excitedly wrapped the present. She carefully placed it under the tree when she was finished. The toy for her brother would definitely excite her brother. They could play with the toy happily all day. Josie's brother was going to be surprised on Christmas!

Assessment 9 – Pronoun/Antecedent Agreement (Lesson 21)
A. Circle the *pronoun* **that agrees with the underlined antecedent.**
1. Marshal washes {his} laundry on Saturdays.
2. The zookeeper forgot {her} hat at home.
3. Cows went to sleep in {their} barn.
4. In Casey's room, {she} found {her} socks.
5. Darla doesn't like {her} soup.
6. The dog wiped {its} paws on the mat.
7. Ariel swam in {her} pool all day.
8. The monkey picked bugs off {its} friend.
9. The doctor forgot {his} stethoscope.
10. I can't believe {my} shoes are already dirty.

B. Complete the sentences with *pronouns.* **Use pronouns that agree with (or match) the underlined antecedents.**
1. The dinosaur ate his **OR** her **OR** its food.
2. Joseph went to the beach in his Jeep. He saw sharks in the sea!
3. That kangaroo jumped so high, his **OR** her **OR** its head touched the tree branch!
4. Kelsey, Rick, and Thomas are siblings. They get along so well.
5. When Tyler lost his action figure, he cried all week.
6. Last year, I went to Disney World and met Minnie Mouse. She was so nice!
7. I saw a mother duck swimming in the pond. She had six babies with her!
8. Ryland and Denise ran a marathon. They were the first pair to finish!

9. My brother was a great writer. He won three awards last year.
10. At the dentist, my sister waited quietly. She got to choose a lollipop!

Assessment 10 – Subject/Verb Agreement (Lesson 22)
A. Circle the *verb* **that agrees with the subject.**
1. Lily {visits} her grandma on Fridays.
2. They {like} to read together.
3. They {bake} chocolate chip cookies.
4. Lily and her grandma {sing} silly songs.
5. Her grandma {sits} in a rocking chair.
6. Lily {rests} on the carpet.

B. Fill in the blanks with verbs. Remember to match *singular subjects* **with** *singular verbs* **and** *plural subjects* **with** *plural verbs*!
Answers may vary.
1. Sheep eat grass.
2. The vet helps 24 animals.
3. My brothers play video games sometimes.
4. Snow lands on the house.
5. The apples fall off the tree.
6. Riley and Leslie walk to the ice cream store.
7. Her pecan pies taste delicious!

C. Circle the *subject* **that agrees with the verb.**
1. {Squids} have huge eyes.
2. The {bear} sleeps in the cave.
3. {The fireman} works very hard.
4. The {plant} is growing so tall!
5. {Cake} bakes in the oven.
6. The {forest} is full of many trees.

Assessment 11 – Contractions & Don't/Doesn't Problem (Lessons 23-24)
A. Underline the *contractions* **in the sentences below. Write the two words that are being combined on the blanks.**
1. You're not at home right now.   you are
2. The turkeys don't fly very often.   do not
3. She'd go to Tennessee if she could.   she would
4. Aren't you going to the movie?   are not
5. There's my lost shoe!   there is

B. Rewrite the sentences and combine the two underlined words into a *contraction.*
1. You've been to Canada five times.
2. Casey knows I'll clean my room.
3. It's going to be so fun going to the fair!
4. My brother won't eat pickles.

C. Write *don't* **or** *doesn't* **to complete the sentence.**
1. My cat doesn't like eating tuna.
2. Charlie and Ann don't go to musicals very often.
3. His friend doesn't have to mow the lawn.
4. The bakers don't always bake bread on Fridays.
5. Their swim coach doesn't feel good today.

Assessment 12 – Writing Sentences in a Series (Lesson 28)
A. Add the missing *commas* **to the** *series* **in the sentences below.**
1. Twizzlers, Skittles, and Twix are my favorite candies.
2. My cousin has a cat, a pig, and a parrot.
3. We hiked, biked, and camped together.
4. They had spaghetti, bread sticks, and broccoli for dinner.
5. Did you read, play, or sleep?

B. Fill in the blanks below with nouns. Add the missing *commas.*
Answers may vary.
1. While we were on vacation, we went to the beach, a museum, and a play.
2. My favorite animals are hippos, lions, and dogs.
3. They had lobster, pasta, and biscuits at the restaurant.
4. Carol wrote a story about animals, airplanes, and volcanos.
5. Roses, tulips, and sunflowers are my friend's favorite flowers.
6. Delilah went to Disney World, the Bahamas, and Texas.

ASSESSMENT ANSWER KEY

C. Fill in the blanks below with verbs. Add the missing *commas*.
Answers may vary.
1. The puppies in the box <u>barked, yipped,</u> and <u>squirmed</u>.
2. In the morning, birds <u>twitter, chirp,</u> and <u>sing</u>.
3. I <u>swim, eat,</u> and <u>watch TV</u> at Grandma's house.
4. In the video game, you <u>hide, hunt,</u> and <u>run</u>.
5. The box <u>tumbled, bounced,</u> and <u>fell</u> down the steps.
6. Food <u>sizzled, cooked,</u> and <u>smoked</u> on the grill.

Assessment 13 – Simple and Compound Sentences (Lesson 29)
A. Identify the following sentences as *simple* or *compound*. If the sentence is simple, write an "S"; if it is compound, write a "C."
1. C
2. S
3. S
4. C
5. S

B. Combine the sentences below using a *comma* and a *conjunction*.
Answers may vary.
1. The dinosaur was tired, so he went to sleep.
2. My cup was empty, but we were out of juice.
3. Heather's room was clean, so her chores were done.
4. We saw Rachel at the store, and we saw Cindy, too.
5. You can paint a picture, or you can make something with clay.

C. Circle the *simple sentences* and underline the *compound sentences*.
1. {Barb was very kind to her friends.}
2. <u>The kangaroo was tired, so he took a nap.</u>
3. {I wore my jacket in the snow.}
4. <u>My cousin plays basketball, but he wants to play soccer.</u>
5. <u>My little wagon broke, so my grandpa fixed it.</u>

Assessment 14 – Incomplete Sentences & Run-On Sentences (Lessons 30-31)
A. The sentences below are *incomplete*. Write "S" if the sentences are missing a *subject* and "P" if they are missing a *predicate*.
1. P
2. P
3. S
4. P

B. Correct the *incomplete sentences* on the line provided.
Answers may vary.
1. Sasha ate nachos with cheese and salsa.
2. Sammy jumped into the freezing lake.

C. Correct each *run-on sentence* by making it into two separate sentences. Don't forget to use *correct punctuation* and *capitalization*.
1. My dad likes sports. His favorite is basketball.
2. My cousin likes dragons. He has three dragon costumes.

D. Correct the *run-on sentence* by making it into a compound sentence. Don't forget to a *comma* and a *conjunction*.
1. Kenny got new boots, and they are very shiny.
2. Krysta likes chips, so she eats them every day.

Unit 1 Comprehensive Assessment (Lessons 2-31)
Circle the letter next to the correct answer.
1. B
2. A
3. B
4. C
5. B
6. C
7. D
8. C
9. B
10. A
11. D
12. A
13. B
14. C
15. B
16. D
17. C

Unit Two: Assessment Answer Key

Assessment 15 – The Writing Process (Lessons 32-37)
Circle the letter next to the correct answer.
1. D
2. B
3. C
4. C

Assessment 16 – Paragraphs (Lessons 38-43)
Circle the letter next to the correct answer.
1. D
2. B
3. D

Assessment 17 – Expository Writing (Lessons 44-53)
Circle the letter next to the correct answer
1. A
2. B
3. B
4. A

Assessment 18 – Persuasive Writing (Lessons 54-63)
Circle the letter next to the correct answer.
1. B
2. D
3. A
4. B

Assessment 19 – Descriptive Writing (Lessons 64-73)
Circle the letter next to the correct answer.
1. C
2. D
3. A
4. C

Unit 2 Comprehensive Assessment (Lessons 32-73)
Circle the letter next to the correct answer
1. C
2. D
3. C
4. A
5. A
6. A
7. D
8. A
9. B
10. B
11. C
12. D
13. C
14. A
15. C
16. C
17. A